Kids On Earth

A Children's Documentary Series Exploring Human Culture & The Natural World

Zimbabwe

Sensei Paul David

Copyright Page

Kids On Earth - A Children's Documentary Series Exploring Global Cultures & The Natural World: Zimbabwe
by Sensei Paul David,

Copyright © 2022.

All rights reserved.

978-1-77848-123-9 KoE_Zimbabwe_Ingram_HardbackBook
978-1-77848-122-2 KoE_Zimbabwe_Ingram_PaperbackBook
978-1-77848-121-5 KoE_Zimbabwe_Amazon_PaperbackBook
978-1-77848-120-8 KoE_Zimbabwe_Amazon_eBook

This book is not authorized for free distribution copying.

www.senseipublishing.com

@senseipublishing
#senseipublishing

Get Our FREE Books Now!

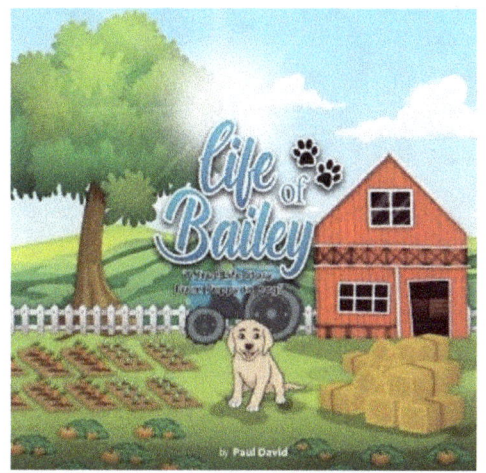

lifeofbailey.senseipublishing.com

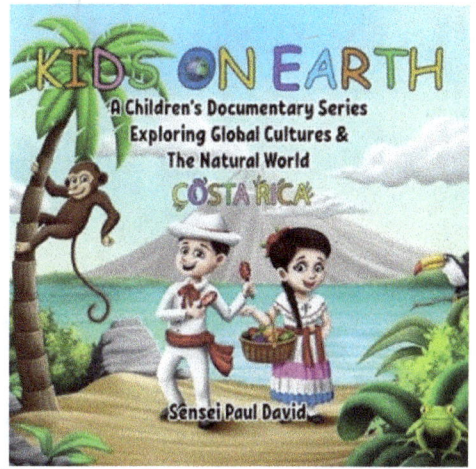

kidsonearth.senseipublishing.com

Click Below or Search Amazon for Another Book In Each Series Or Visit:

www.amazon.com/author/senseipauldavid

Join Our Publishing Journey!

If you would like to receive FUTURE FREE BOOKS and get to know us better, please click www.senseipublishing.com and join our newsletter by entering your email address in the pop-up box.

Follow Our Blog: senseipauldavid.ca

Follow/Like/Subscribe: Facebook, Instagram, YouTube: @senseipublishing

Scan the QR Code with your phone or tablet to follow us on social media:

Like / Subscribe / Follow

Good day, everybody, and welcome to Zimbabwe! My name is Kutenda, and this is my younger sister Danai. We live in the capital city of Zimbabwe called Harare. Have you heard of it?

Zimbabwe is a landlocked country in Southern Africa. It is one of the most beautiful places to visit, and Danai and I can't wait to show you around our wonderful home.

Are you ready to see the biggest waterfall in the world? How about exploring one of the most important ancient African cities? Would you like to see lions and giraffes on safari in the Hwange National Park? There is so much to see in Zimbabwe, so grab your walking shoes, and let's get exploring!

FUN FACTS
A landlocked country has no coastlines and is surrounded by other countries. Zimbabwe shares a border with South Africa, Mozambique, Botswana, and Zambia.

Zimbabwe is a small country that is about the same size as California. We have two major cities in our country, and Danai and I live in one of them.

We live in Harare. Harare is the biggest city in Zimbabwe. It is also our capital city, which means that there are many government buildings and historic buildings around our home. There are also lots of tall modern skyscrapers in Harare.

We have cousins who live in Bulawayo. Bulawayo is a large city in the south of the country. It is the second largest and second most populated city in the country. People first moved here in 1840.

FUN FACTS

Harare is home to 1.5 million people, while only 700 thousand people live in Bulawayo.

There are a few other big cities here too. They include Mutare, Epworth, and Gweru. These cities are a lot smaller than Harare and Bulawayo, and each has less than 200 thousand people living in them.

We have a subtropical climate here in Zimbabwe, but the weather can be very different from one side of the country to another. Summer is from October to March, which is also our rainy season. It is hot and rainy during summer, and there are a lot of thunderstorms with bright lightning and thunder.

Our winter is from June to September. During winter, it is warm during the day and cools at night. This is also the driest time of the year.

In the south of the country, it is very hot and dry. The middle of the country experiences cold weather in winter. It doesn't snow in the cities, but sometimes, there is a lot of frost on the ground.

FUN FACTS

Because we have long, dry winters, we get a lot of droughts here in Southern Africa. A drought happens when there is not enough rain in the wet months to last through the dry months. Many crops and animals die during droughts because there is not enough water to drink.

I think it is very interesting that we get more rain in Summer than in Winter. What do you think about this?

There are so many things that make our country unique. We have some of the friendliest and most hard-working people in the world here. Our government does not have much money, and much of our population is poor. This means that those lucky enough to have a job work very hard to prove themselves.

Our diverse population also makes us very special. Many different indigenous groups and tribes call the country home. These populations have influenced the history and culture of Zimbabwe over thousands of years.

FUN FACTS

An indigenous group is a tribe of people who have been living in a place for a long time.

In fact, during the 13th and 14th centuries, Zimbabwe was one of the greatest African civilizations. You can visit the ruins of these ancient cities today - but more on that later!

Not only do we have amazing people here, but we also have some of the most beautiful landscapes and diverse wildlife in the world.

Have you heard of Victoria Falls? It is the biggest waterfall in the world and is very beautiful to visit. Victoria Falls is on the Zambezi River, which runs between Zimbabwe and Zambia. You can even go bungee-jumping and white-water rafting in this river!

FUN FACTS

We call the waterfall 'The Smoke That Thunders' because of the loud sound the water makes.

You can also take a trip to Lake Kariba, the largest man-made lake in the world. We stay in a houseboat on Lake Kariba every year with our families. Sometimes, we even see some crocodiles and hippos in the lake.

Lake Kariba is used to create hydroelectric power for Zambia and Zimbabwe. Hydropower is a type of renewable energy that creates electricity using moving water. We are proud of our government for making our electricity out of the natural resources we have in our country.

Because we have no sea here, we also farm fish in the lake, which we eat across the country. Our main fish are tilapia, kapenta, and tigerfish.

FUN FACTS

A man-made lake is a lake that people dig using big machines. Countries usually do this to create space to store water for people to use and drink. Unfortunately, the water levels of Lake Kariba have gone down because of our dry droughts.

Renewable energy is a type of energy that uses natural resources that can be easily replaced. For example, some types of renewable energy use the sun, wind, and water to create electricity. Creating electricity using renewable energy is good for our environment.

Can you believe over 15 million people are living in Zimbabwe? This might sound like a lot, but we don't have a huge population for such a big country.

About 68% live in rural towns and settlements, and only 32% live in urban centers. Rural areas include the countryside and farms where people live in homes far away from each other.

Urban areas include big cities like Harare and Bulawayo. Here, we live closer to our neighbors and have less space to run around.

FUN FACTS

California is the same size as Zimbabwe and has about 40 million people living there. Zimbabwe has less than half the number of people that California has!

For a long time, our country used to be called Rhodesia. It got this name from a British man called Cecil John Rhodes, who colonized the land. Rhodesia was a British colony from 1890 to 1980.

Colonization is when a group of people from one country take over and build their homes in another place that might not be theirs to take. Because European countries had invented guns and deadly weapons earlier than Africa, they took control of a lot of African lands without permission. We are still living with the effects of colonization in our country.

Zimbabwe got its name from the Shona word for 'House in Stone,' which has to do with the Great Zimbabwe ruins and the ancient people who lived there.

FUN FACTS

Rhodesia was renamed Zimbabwe in 1980 when we gained independence from our colonial rulers.

Long before Zimbabwe was known as Rhodesia, the land we live on was known as Matabeleland and Mashonaland.

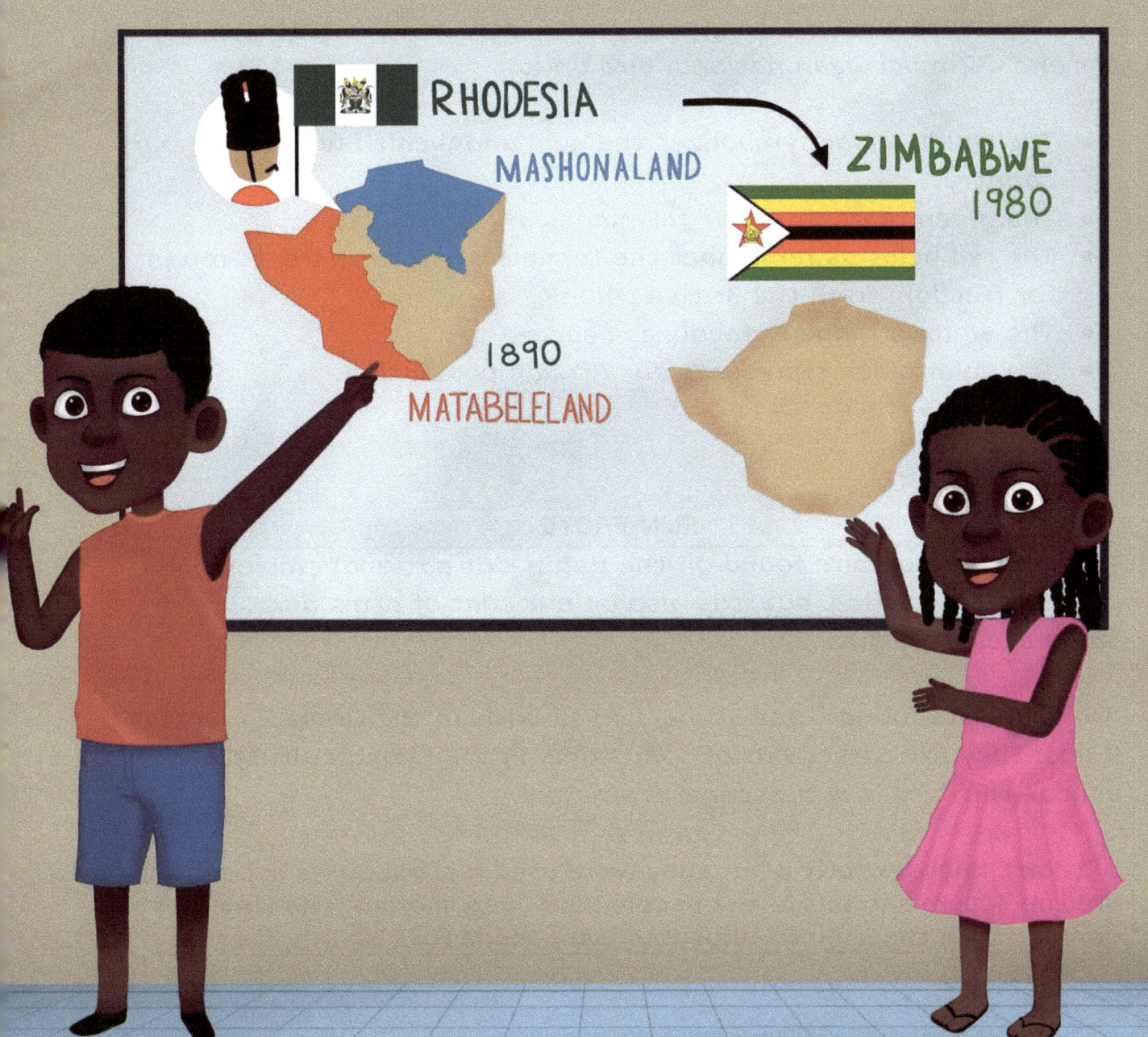

When we got our new country name, we also got a new flag! The Zimbabwean flag has seven green, yellow, red, and black stripes with a star and a Zimbabwean national bird on it.

- The yellow color symbolizes the gold and wealth we have in our country.
- The green represents our farmlands and agriculture.
- The red helps us remember the terrible wars our parents fought for freedom from the British colony.
- The white triangle symbolizes peace.
- The color black represents our African population.

FUN FACTS

The Zimbabwean bird found on the flag is our national emblem! Not only is it on our flag, but it is also on our coat of arms and our banknotes and coins.

Archeologists found these stone-carved birds in the Great Zimbabwe Ruins. They are carved out of soapstone. In the Shona culture, we believe this bird is a messenger from God.

We don't know exactly what they were used for, but some believe they are the Totem animals of the people who lived there at the time. What do you think these bird sculptures were made for?

Because there are so many different tribes in Zimbabwe, we have a very diverse culture. Danai and I are from the Shona tribe. Most of the people here are Shona.

We believe in a God called Mwari and have a lot of traditions to ask our ancestors for good health, rain, and success. We also believe in spirits and magic. We believe that good and evil spirits can make good things happen.

FUN FACTS

The Shona tribe is the largest ethnic group in Zimbabwe. There are five different Shona sub-tribes. They are the Zezuru, Karanda, Manyika, Tonga-Korekore and Ndau.

80% of the people in Southern Africa are Shona. We also have many tribe members who live in Botswana, Mozambique, Zambia, and South Africa.

Although Danai and I live in the city with our family, many of our Shona cousins live in the countryside in huts made with mud walls and thatch roofs. Some important parts of our culture are ironwork, pottery, and music. We also love to create beautiful art and music with our friends and family.

The Shona people believe in the power of Totems. A Totem is usually a different animal that is linked to a specific person. For example, a strong man might have a lion Totem, which he will pass down to his children from generation to generation.

FUN FACTS

Each Shona group has a connection to a different Totem. Danai and my family's Totem is the Monkey, known as the 'Soko.'

Our Totem tribe is like our family, and when we are old enough to get married, we are not allowed to marry someone with the same Totem as us. What Totem do you think your family would have?

One of the other main tribes in Zimbabwe is the Ndebele tribe. This tribe lives around Bulawayo and Southern Zimbabwe, and in our neighboring country South Africa.

Ndebele people live in round huts which they paint using bright colors and patterns. They are very beautiful to look at! They build their homes in a circle to surround and protect their farm animals.

FUN FACTS

A long time ago, the Ndebele people used to be called the Matabele tribe.

When a Ndebele woman gets married, her husband's family must pay her family with cows and livestock.

We dress beautifully here in Zimbabwe. In the cities, most of us wear Western clothes as you wear. But for special occasions, we wear our traditional Shona outfits.

Traditional Shona clothing is made from animal skins called 'mhapa' and 'shashiko.' Today, we wear a lot of clothing made from cloth material called Tsonga.

People from the Ndebele tribe wear different outfits to us. Married women wrap a colorful blanket around their shoulders and wear headdresses decorated with colorful beads. They wear a lot of hand-beaded jewelry and brass bangles around their necks and arms.

FUN FACTS

The blanket that married Ndebele women wear is called a 'Nguba.' It is common for a bride to get a Nguba as a gift on her wedding day.

In the rural parts of the country, many tribes wear their traditional clothing every day.

We have five UNESCO World Heritage Sites here in Zimbabwe. Two of them are natural, and three are cultural.

The ruins of Great Zimbabwe are one of the most popular tourist attractions in the country. They are the ruins of an ancient city that used to be home to the Queen of Sheba, who ruled over much of Southern Africa.

Our Shona ancestors used to live here between the 11th and 15th centuries. Can you imagine what life was like 1000 years ago? Our ancestors who lived here traded gold that they mined in the area and lived a good life.

Eventually, the city grew too big, and too many people needed to be fed. As the food ran out in Great Zimbabwe, many people left and settled in the City of Khami, now known as the Khami Ruins.

FUN FACTS

A UNESCO World Heritage Site is a special place with important meaning for a country, which is protected by the government.

A few items have been found around Great Zimbabwe that prove that our ancestors traded with China and Persia.

Victoria Falls and Mana Pools National Park are our two natural World Heritage Sites. Mana Pools National Park is a beautiful place where lots of wildlife live. Many people visit this national park on safari to see the animals in their natural habitat.

The Matobo Hills are another important World Heritage Site and cultural place for the Shona people.

There are a lot of important rock paintings on the granite rocks here. Some of this rock art is as old as 13 thousand years! These paintings of people and animals tell us a lot about the people who lived in the area thousands of years ago.

The hills are very beautiful, and many of our friends and family believe they are connected to God and our ancestors. There are even a few sacred shrines around the hills where people can go to make contact with the spiritual world.

FUN FACTS

The Matobo Hills are near the city of Bulawayo, and the area is now a National Park that the government protects. This means that people can't build on this land or take anything away from it.

Cecil John Rhodes was buried at the Matobo Hills when he died in 1902.

We follow the Christian religion here in Zimbabwe. In fact, more than 80% of the people here are Christian too. We like to think of ourselves as Syncretic Christians. This means we follow part of the Christian religion and part of our own tribal beliefs.

Our religion plays a big role in our education and everyday life. Danai and I learn about our Christian religion at school.

FUN FACTS

When Zimbabwe was an English colony, many people would come here to teach our ancestors about Christianity. This is why so many of us follow this religion today. Before this time, our ancestors would follow our traditional Shona and Ndebele beliefs.

Shona and Ndebele's traditional religious practices were quite similar. We both believe in a God and worship our ancestors.

In our Shona religion, we pray to Mwari (our God) to ask for help and guidance when we have problems.

Can you believe that there are sixteen official languages in Zimbabwe? Danai and I speak Shona as our first language. Over 70% of our population can speak this language, and 20% of Zimbabweans speak Ndebele. The other 10% speak other national languages such as Chewa, Kalanga, and Sotho.

English is also one of the national languages of Zimbabwe, and most of us can understand English pretty well. This means that you won't struggle to chat with us when you visit Zimbabwe.

If you visit us in Harare, you will mostly hear people speaking Shona. But when you visit Bulawayo, you will hear more Ndebele.

FUN FACTS

Both Shona and Ndebele are Bantu languages. This means that they were first spoken by Bantu-speaking tribes over 10 thousand years ago.

When you visit us in Zimbabwe, you might want to learn a few phrases in Shona. Why don't you write these on a piece of paper and carry them with you when you travel?

- Hello - Mhoro
- Thank you - Waita hako
- How are you? - Wakadini?
- Do you speak English? - Unotaura Chirungu?
- Can you help me? - Ungandibatsirawo here?
- I don't understand - Handisi kunzwisisa

FUN FACTS

Just like in the English language, we have a different way to say hello at different times of the day:

- Good morning - Mangwanani Mangwanani
- Good afternoon - Masikati Masikati
- Good evening - Manheru Maswere

Zimbabwe is rich in natural resources. Natural resources can be found underneath the ground and are worth a lot of money.

Zimbabwe's main natural resources are gold, coal, nickel, copper, iron, lithium, tin, and platinum. These are special metals that we can sell for a high price. We even have diamonds here in Zimbabwe!

Mining is our biggest industry. We dig deep underground using big machines and find gold in rocks. We make a lot of money from the gold that we mine by selling it to other countries around the world.

FUN FACTS

Mining played an important role in building the country. Our natural resources and hard-working people helped bring a lot of money into the country to pay to build our cities and feed our people. Mining has also created a lot of important jobs.

We also export a lot of cotton, tobacco, and clothing, which talented people sew here in Zimbabwe.

Exporting is when countries sell resources that they have to other countries to make money. Importing is when we bring things into our country which we do not naturally have.

Unfortunately, the story of our economy and money is a sad one. Before Danai and I were born, Zimbabwe used to have a lot of money from all the natural resources and mines.

At this time, our parents used the Zimbabwean Dollar to buy things. This was their national currency, and it was worth a lot of money. But then, a greedy government took all of our people's hard-earned money for themselves. We call this a corrupt government.

Today, we use the United States Dollar as our main currency, and our economy is in a very bad way.

FUN FACTS

Most Zimbabweans work in the agricultural, mining, and manufacturing sectors. The agricultural sector includes all the farmers who work their fields for crops and livestock. Those who work in the manufacturing sector spend their days building furniture and sewing clothing.

Tourism is another big sector in Zimbabwe, and we make a lot of money from all the people who visit Victoria Falls and come here on safari every year.

We have a semi-presidential republic here in Zimbabwe, which means we have a president and a prime minister.

Our new president was elected in 2018. All of our parents and older siblings went to vote in what we call a general election.

The new President of Zimbabwe will be in office for five years before we elect a new president into power. Did you know that you have to be over the age of 18 to vote for our president? I can't wait until I can join my parents and vote when I am older!

FUN FACTS

Until our country gained independence in 1980, the white colonialist government had control over our people. During this time, the black population in Zimbabwe had very few rights.

In a semi-presidential government, both the president and the prime minister manage the country's politics.

We have an amazing ecosystem here in Zimbabwe. Most of the country is a savanna landscape. A savanna is a tropical grassland landscape where plants can grow in hot and dry weather.

Trees are spread out across a dry area that is overgrown with tall grasses and shrubs. This is the perfect landscape for wildlife and is very common across the African continent.

FUN FACTS

Because there isn't too much rain in the savanna, animals often have to travel far to find water holes.

A water hole is a small body of water where lots of trees and plants grow and where animals drink and bathe. When you go on safari, water holes are the best place to find beautiful animals.

Because we have a subtropical climate, there are areas in Zimbabwe that are very lush and green.

Near the eastern border of the country, there are a few evergreen forests with tall teak trees. An evergreen tree is a tree that doesn't lose its green leaves during winter and is green throughout the year.

We also have a very special tree called the baobab in Zimbabwe. In fact, there are about 5 million baobab trees across the country. These trees have thick trunks and can live with very little water.

FUN FACTS

There are a lot of green trees and tropical plants around the Zambezi River, Victoria Falls, and Lake Kariba.

Danai's favorite tree is the jacaranda. This is a beautiful tree with thousands of bright purple flowers that bloom twice a year during spring and fall. The streets in Harare are lined with these beautiful purple trees!

Baobab tree

Jacaranda tree

Zimbabwe is known for being home to the Big 5. The Big 5 are the most famous animals to see on safari: the lion, African elephant, buffalo, leopard, and rhinoceros.

You can also see many hippopotamuses, giraffes, hyenas, and wild dogs in the African savanna. We have many different types of bucks in Zimbabwe. A buck is an animal with horns, similar to a deer. Our most famous species are the kudu, duiker, impala, steenbok and antelope. Have you heard of any of these animals before?

If you're very lucky, you might even see a cheetah. They are very hard to find and like to hide away from humans. Cheetahs are Danai's favorite animals!

FUN FACTS
Most of Zimbabwe's wildlife lives in the Hwange National Park. So, when you visit us in Zimbabwe, make sure you visit the African savanna and go on a once-in-a-lifetime safari adventure.

Many Zimbabweans work to help keep our animals and national parks safe. Unfortunately, some people like to hunt our animals for their skin, horns, or tusks, which they sell overseas for a lot of money.

Special people called conservationists help protect our animals from unfriendly humans. They live with our animals to make sure they are always safe. We are very thankful for these amazing people.

FUN FACTS

Do you know what conservation is? Wildlife conservation is when people help protect animals from becoming endangered.

There are also a lot of non-governmental organizations that help keep our national parks from being turned into big cities. For our animals to survive, we need to protect their homes.

A non-governmental organization is a group of people who does work without expecting to be paid for it. They are very important in Africa, where many countries and people do not have enough money to help themselves.

You can find some of the most interesting insects here in Zimbabwe. We have some beautiful beetles which have bright shiny colors.

There are over seven hundred different species of birds flying around our country. We have ostriches, ducks, geese, doves, and flamingoes.

My favorite bird is called the Fish Eagle. It is the same bird that we have on our national flag and is our national bird. It is a huge eagle with wide wings, and it is very good at catching fish.

FUN FACTS

Don't be too quick to jump into the water at Lake Kariba, because some hippopotamuses and crocodiles are living here!

One of the most famous insects in Zimbabwe is the mopane worm. Did you know that we eat this worm as a tasty treat? Today, you can even order mopane worms in a restaurant in big cities.

Fish Eagle

Ostrich

Flamingo

Duck

Geese

52

We eat some delicious food here in Zimbabwe. Would you like to have a taste? For most meals, we eat sadza, which is a grain made from white corn. Sadza is the staple food of Zimbabwe, and it is usually eaten with meat stew and green vegetables.

Yellow watermelon is a traditional Ndebele dish that we sometimes eat when we visit our Ndebele friends. They boil the watermelon and beat it into a porridge with sun-dried maize and sugar. Have you ever seen a yellow watermelon?

FUN FACTS

White corn is grown across the country. Aside from helping to feed our people, we sell a lot of our maize to other countries. We also grow a lot of groundnuts, beans, and sorghum here.

A staple food crop is a type of food that is traditionally eaten every day. Different countries have different staple foods, depending on what grows best on their land.

I love to play football with my friends after school. Football is the most popular sport in the country, but we also enjoy playing rugby and cricket!

If you like to play basketball, netball, water polo, or chess, you will fit right in here!

FUN FACTS

Our people are very fast and strong and have won eight Olympic medals! We love watching Zimbabweans play in the Olympic Games every four years.

Dance and music are very important to our culture. There are about twelve different traditional dances that we like to dance on special occasions. My favorite is the Mbira Dance, and Danai loves to watch the Shangara Dance!

FUN FACTS

Our traditional dances help teach us about our history and different important life values. They are a way to tell stories, and we like to dance at special religions and social events like weddings and religious holidays.

Musicians often play beautiful music when we dance. The most famous Zimbabwean instrument is the mbira, which is a string instrument used during many religious rituals.

Mbira Dance

Shangara Dance

Danai and I had such a wonderful time showing you around our beautiful home country, and we hope you enjoyed the journey as much as we did!

Our people are friendly, and we follow interesting traditions.
We are hard-working and care about our animals and land.
Our culture is very diverse, and traditions are important to us.
We have some of the most exciting wildlife living around us.
We love to play sports and spend time outside in the sunshine.

We hope you learned a bit about our country, people, animals, and traditions, and we can't wait to welcome you back to Zimbabwe soon!

Musare zvakanaka!

Visit us at www.senseipublishing.com and sign up for our newsletter to learn more about our exciting books and to experience our **FREE Guided Meditations for Kids & Adults.**

As always...

It's a great day to be alive!

What have you learned?

Take this quiz to see how much you have learned about Kutenda and Danai's home country!

1) How many people live in Harare?
    a) 1.5 million people
    b) 700 thousand
    c) 3 million people
    d) 400 thousand people

2) How much of the population lives in rural towns and settlements?
    a) 25%
    b) 68%
    c) 30%
    d) 100%

3) What American State is Zimbabwe a similar size to?
    a) New York
    b) Idaho
    c) Massachusetts
    d) California

4) In what year did Zimbabwe gain independence from the British colony?
    a) 1890
    b) 2000
    c) 1980

d) 1800
5) What does the color yellow represent on Zimbabwe's national flag?
   a) Gold and money
   b) Peace
   c) The African population
   d) Farming and agriculture

6) What currency do Zimbabweans use today?
   a) The United States Dollar
   b) The Zimbabwean Dollar

7) How many World Heritage Sites are there in Zimbabwe?
   a) 0
   b) 6
   c) 2
   d) 5

8) BONUS QUESTION: Which beautiful place would you like to visit first when you visit Kutenda and Danai in Zimbabwe?

Don't forget to share all of the new things you have learned with a friend!

Quiz Answers: 1A, 2B, 3D, 4C, 5A, 6A, 7D

Get/Share Our FREE All-Ages Mental Health Books Now!

lifeofbailey.senseipublishing.com

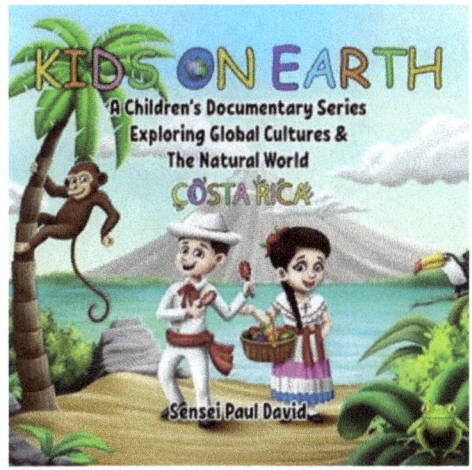

kidsonearth.senseipublishing.com

Click Below or Search Amazon for Another Book In Each Series Or Visit:

www.amazon.com/author/senseipauldavid

www.senseipublishing.com

@senseipublishing
#senseipublishing

Check out our **recommendations** for other books for adults & kids plus other great resources by visiting
www.senseipublishing.com/resources/

Join Our Publishing Journey!

If you would like to receive FREE BOOKS and special offers, please visit www.senseipublishing.com and join our newsletter by entering your email address in the pop-up box

Follow Our Engaging Blog NOW!
senseipauldavid.ca

Get Our FREE Books Today!

Click & Share the Links Below

FREE Kids Books

lifeofbailey.senseipublishing.com
kidsonearth.senseipublishing.com

FREE Self-Development Book

senseiselfdevelopment.senseipublishing.com

FREE BONUS!!!
Experience Over 25 FREE Engaging Guided Meditations!

Prized Skills & Practices for Adults & Kids. Help Restore Deep Sleep, Lower Stress, Improve Posture, Navigate Uncertainty & More.

Download the Free Insight Timer App and click the link below:
http://insig.ht/sensei_paul

About Sensei Publishing

Sensei Publishing commits itself to help people of all ages transform into better versions of themselves by providing high-quality and research-based self-development books with an emphasis on mental health and guided meditations. Sensei Publishing offers well-written e-books, audiobooks, paperbacks and online courses that simplify complicated but practical topics in line with its mission to inspire people towards positive transformation.

It's a great day to be alive!

About the Author

I create simple & transformative eBooks & Guided Meditations for Adults & Children proven to help navigate uncertainty, solve niche problems & bring families closer together.

I'm a former finance project manager, private pilot, jiu-jitsu instructor, musician & former University of Toronto Fitness Trainer. I prefer a science-based approach to focus on these & other areas in my life to stay humble & hungry to evolve. I hope you enjoy my work and I'd love to hear your feedback.

- It's a great day to be alive!
Sensei Paul David

Scan & Follow/Like/Subscribe: Facebook, Instagram, YouTube: @senseipublishing

Scan using your phone/iPad camera for Social Media
Visit us at www.senseipublishing.com and sign up for our newsletter to learn more about our exciting books and to experience our FREE Guided Meditations for Kids & Adults.

www.ingramcontent.com/pod-product-compliance
Lightning Source LLC
Chambersburg PA
CBHW080605170426
43209CB00007B/1336